C000243265

IMAGES OF WAR

617 DAMBUSTER SQUADRON AT WAR

IMAGES OF WAR
617 DAMBUSTER SQUADRON AT WAR

RARE PHOTOGRAPHS FROM WARTIME ARCHIVES

CHRIS WARD and ANDY LEE

Pen & Sword
AVIATION

First published in Great Britain in 2009 by
PEN & SWORD AVIATION
an imprint of
Pen & Sword Books Ltd,
47 Church Street, Barnsley,
South Yorkshire.
S70 2AS

Copyright © Chris Ward and Andy Lee, 2009

ISBN 978-1-84884-002-7

The right of Chris Ward and Andy Lee to be identified as Authors of
this Work has been asserted by them in accordance with the
Copyright, Designs and Patents Act 1988.

A CIP catalogue record for this book is available
from the British Library

*All rights reserved. No part of this book may be reproduced or transmitted
in any form or by any means, electronic or mechanical including photocopying,
recording or by any information storage and retrieval system,
without permission from the Publisher in writing.*

Typeset by Mac Style, Beverley, East Yorkshire
Printed and bound in Great Britain by CPI

Pen & Sword Books Ltd incorporates the imprints of
Pen & Sword Aviation, Pen & Sword Maritime,
Pen & Sword Military, Pen & Sword Select, Pen & Sword Military Classics,
Leo Cooper, Wharncliffe Local History

For a complete list of Pen & Sword titles please contact:
PEN & SWORD BOOKS LIMITED
47 Church Street, Barnsley, South Yorkshire, S70 2AS, England.
E-mail: enquiries@pen-and-sword.co.uk
Website: www.pen-and-sword.co.uk

Guy Penrose Gibson was born in India on the 12th of August 1918. His father was a member of the Indian Forestry Service, resident in Simla, the summer administrative centre. The young Gibson was sent home to England in 1924 to begin his education, which would progress over the ensuing years in an adequate but undistinguished manner. In November 1936 he began initial training as a Royal Air Force pilot, and passed out with an average assessment before joining 83 Squadron, a bomber unit, at Turnhouse in September 1937. When war came two years later, Gibson was a Pilot Officer. He carried out his first operational sortie on the day war broke out, but had to wait until the fall of the Low Countries before his war service gained momentum. He eventually departed 83 Squadron in September 1940 after 39 operations. Volunteering for a tour on night fighters to remain on active service, he joined 29 Squadron, flying 99 sorties during the next 12 months during which time he destroyed 3 enemy aircraft. At the end of June 1941, during this period of service, he was promoted to the rank of Squadron Leader. His wish to return to bomber operations was granted in March 1942, when he was given command of 5 Group's 106 Squadron.

This posed photograph of Gibson was taken on the 22nd of July 1943, two months after Operation *Chastise*, and less than two weeks before his departure from 617 Squadron to join Churchill's party on a tour of America. The picture is one of a series of images of him and his crew. What looks like an idyllic meadow is in fact the main airfield just across the perimeter track from the 617 Squadron hangar. After a highly successful twelve months in command of 106 Squadron, during which he carried out 28 operations, (ORB) or 29 (logbook), Gibson was specifically chosen by ACM Harris, C-in-C Bomber Command, to form the new Squadron to attack Germany's dams. He took up his appointment at Scampton in March 1943, returning to the station where his war had begun with 83 Squadron. He was just 24 years of age when given the enormous responsibility of building a squadron to carry such high expectations. Contrary to the perpetuated myth, Gibson did not hand pick every member of aircrew, or even the pilots. He was, though, able to select some with whom he had served during his 106 Squadron days, and others whom he knew within the Group. Following the successful, if expensive foray against the Möhne, Eder and Sorpe Dams, Gibson was awarded the Victoria Cross to add to the DSO and Bar and DFC and Bar gained earlier in his distinguished operational career.

Gibson is pictured here meeting Sir Archibald Sinclair, Secretary of State for Air, at 54 Base Coningsby on the 3rd of September 1944, just two weeks before his untimely death. Also present is Air Commodore "Bobby" Sharpe, the base commander. During the spring of 1944, 5 Group became largely autonomous through the introduction of its own target marking force. The heavy element of this, comprising 83 and 97 Squadrons, was based at Coningsby. At the time Gibson was Senior Air Staff Officer (SASO) on this station that was home to 5 Group's Master Bomber fraternity. They were a collection of the most experienced bomber pilots in 5 Group, who were given the responsibility of controlling operations from the air in the manner pioneered by Gibson during Operation *Chastise*. Gibson was by now a frustrated man, desperate to get back into the war before it finished, and he had managed to wangle a number of unofficial sorties flying as an additional "bod" with crews from East Kirkby. He had also enjoyed a trip in a Mosquito, the aircraft of choice for 5 Group's Master Bombers, as well as a Lockheed Lightning, a type being evaluated as a possible alternative. When offered the opportunity to act as Master Bomber on an operation to the twin towns of Mönchengladbach and Rheydt on the night of the 19/20th September, he grabbed it with both hands. Despite some difficulties with a

complex target marking plan, the operation was concluded successfully, and Gibson was heard to direct the crews to head for home. On the way back his Mosquito came down on the edge of the town of Steenbergen in southern Holland, and he and his navigator, S/L Jim Warwick were killed. The most likely cause of the crash was fuel starvation through the crew members' lack of familiarity with the Mosquito and its fuel transfer procedures.

A Lancaster modified to Type 464 Provisioning requirements for delivery of the Barnes Wallis designed *Upkeep* dambusting bomb. ED825/G was a trials aircraft pictured here at Boscombe Down. This aircraft was the only one of the modified batch to incorporate a ventral gun position. The gun barrel can be seen protruding beneath the fuselage between the roundel and serial number. Flown to Scampton on the afternoon of Sunday 16th May, the day on which Operation *Chastise* was launched, this aircraft was pressed into service as AJ-T and flown to the Sorpe Dam by F/L Joe McCarthy and crew after their ED915 sprang a glycol leak at start-up. There was insufficient time to install the spotlight altimeter system and VHF radio, but the method of attack at the Sorpe made this less critical. ED825 returned safely from Operation *Chastise* and remained with 617 Squadron until failing to return from an operation over France conducted on behalf of the Special Operations Executive (SOE) at Tempsford on the night of the 10/11th December 1943. F/O Weeden and crew lost their lives, and the wreckage of the Lancaster was finally uncovered during filming for a Channel 5 documentary in 2007. This featured "Johnny" Johnson, who was McCarthy's bomb-aimer at the Sorpe, and used Chris Ward's book, *Dambusters, The Definitive History* as its source.

Wing Commander Gibson and F/L "Bob" Hutchison, his wireless operator, are seen here preparing to board ED932 for Operation *Chastise* on the evening of Sunday 16th May 1943. Over his shirt sleeves Gibson is wearing his beloved "Mae West", which he acquired from a shot-down German airman in 1940. Hutchison had previously served with Gibson's former command, 106 Squadron. He was prone to air sickness, but he never allowed the condition to interfere with his operational duties.

Three 617 Squadron stalwarts posing in front of a Lancaster at Scampton during July 1943. On the left is P/O "Bunny" Clayton, one of a number of new pilots posted in to 617 Squadron to replace those lost on Operation *Chastise*. He arrived from 4 Group's 51 Squadron on July 2nd, the same day that S/L George Holden was posted in also from 4 Group as Gibson's intended successor. Clayton would remain with the squadron for twelve months, completing a distinguished second tour. He undertook his final operation on the 25th of June 1944 against a V-Weapon storage site at Siracourt in France, and was posted to 1663 Conversion Unit on July 22nd, by which time he had advanced to the rank of Flight Lieutenant. In the centre is S/L David Maltby, a squadron original, who's *Upkeep* had sealed the fate of the Möhne Dam. Before arriving at Scampton he had served with 97 Squadron at Woodhall Spa. A Flight Lieutenant during the dams period, Maltby was promoted to the rank of Squadron Leader to fill one of the two flight commander posts left vacant by the loss of Young and Maudslay during *Chastise*. Sadly Maltby would not survive the war, unlike F/L Harold "Mick" Martin standing to his left. Martin was an Australian and another 617 Squadron original, who had previously served with 455 Squadron RAAF and 50 Squadron. He would take temporary command of 617 Squadron during its second rebuilding following the disaster of the Dortmund-Ems Canal operation in September 1943, and in 1944 would join 515 Squadron in 100 Group to operate as a Mosquito night fighter pilot hunting down Luftwaffe night fighters.

A royal visit to Scampton took place on Thursday the 27th of May 1943, and here Queen Elizabeth is pictured in conversation with AVM Cochrane, Air-Officer-Commanding 5 Group. At the rear in a formal suit is Dr Barnes Wallis, who had conceived the weapon known as *Upkeep*, or more popularly, the "bouncing bomb", which had been employed so spectacularly against the dams. Wallis expressed surprise at being invited to join the royal party.

Another shot of the royal visit captures King George VI chatting with Gibson, while station commander Air Commodore J.N.H. "Charles" Whitworth keeps pace to their left. In the background stands Gibson's dams Lancaster ED932, with air and ground crew lined up in front. Whitworth was the kind of man to whom Gibson could relate, and was the ideal choice to be his mentor during the build up to Operation *Chastise*. Gibson respected those with operational credentials, and Whitworth was such a man, having served as a Whitley pilot with 10 Squadron early in the war, and then as commanding officer of 51 and 35 Squadrons for brief periods in 1941 and 42.

King George shakes hand with a member of Gibson's ground crew. Barely visible against the backdrop of the air intake of the starboard inner engine, (and best viewed through a magnifying glass), is the forward spotlight, which cast a constant circle of light on the water just ahead of the starboard leading edge during the Lancaster's approached to attack altitude. As the aircraft edged closer to its 60 feet release height the circle from the rear spotlight appeared to move diagonally backwards from right to left until touching the forward circle to form a figure of 8.

Australian Dambusters. F/L "Mickey" Martin poses with four members of his crew during the visit to London for the investiture. From left to right, F/L Jack Leggo from Sydney was the navigator, who had been with Martin from the start. He was awarded a Bar to his DFC for the Dams operation, which was his 35th. At the conclusion of his tour Leggo remustered as a pilot, and flew further operations with an Australian maritime squadron. F/S "Tammy" Simpson from Hobart, Tasmania, flew in Martin's rear turret, and had also served with 455 and 50 Squadrons. He was awarded the coveted DFM for his part in Operation *Chastise*. Like Leggo he would undertake a pilot's course, and ultimately be awarded a DFC in recognition of completing 50 operations. F/L Bob Hay was appointed 617 Squadron's first bombing leader in recognition of his experience, and held that distinction until his untimely death. He served with Martin in both 455 and 50 Squadrons, and at 29 years of age was a little older than the average aircrew member. During an attack on the Antheor Viaduct on France's Riviera coast on the night of the 11/12th of February 1944, Martin's Lancaster was hit by flak shrapnel, and Hay sustained a fatal wound. He is buried on Sardinia, where Martin made an emergency landing after the operation. P/O Toby Foxlee flew on Operation *Chastise* in the front turret of P-Popsie, but he usually occupied the mid-upper position, which was absent on the Dams modified Lancasters. By the time he returned to Australia in July 1944, he had been awarded the DFM and DFC. F/L Harold "Mickey" Martin ended the war with two DSOs and three DFCs. He was brought to Gibson's attention as a man with low-flying experience, and this brought him an invitation to become a founder member of 617 Squadron. The other members of Martin's Dams crew were flight engineer Ivan Whittaker, a Briton, and New Zealander Len Chambers, the wireless operator.

Another gathering of Australian survivors of Operation *Chastise*. This is an unofficial and uncensored photograph, which shows the white whip aerial for VHF communication and the spotlight housing. The official photo has been cropped to remove sensitive material. From L – R. P/O Lance Howard was the navigator in Townsend's crew. He was 30 years of age and hailed from Freemantle, Western Australia. F/L David Shannon was one of those not overawed by Gibson's character, and soon became a member of his inner circle while they served together at 106 Squadron. At the conclusion of his tour Shannon volunteered for Pathfinder training, and had just arrived at Wyton when the call came through from Gibson to join him at Scampton. Between Jack Leggo and Mickey Martin stands Les Knight who was regarded as a gentle and quiet young man, who, but for the war, would have become an accountant in his home state of Victoria. He served with 50 Squadron before being posted to 617 as a founder member. As he made his attack on the Eder Dam, he was aware that his was the last available bomb of the first wave. He made it count by bringing the huge wall crashing down. His Lancaster was one of five out of eight that failed to return from attacking the Dortmund-Ems Canal on the night of the 15/16th of September 1943. He held the stricken Lancaster aloft until his crew had taken to their parachutes, but he died at the controls in an attempted crash-landing in a Dutch field. Standing to his left in the photo is Sgt Bob Kellow, his wireless operator, who, with four others, managed to evade capture and return to the UK.

The Canadians also played a magnificent role in Operation *Chastise*. Here the survivors gather in another unofficial, uncensored photograph. From L – R back row they are Sgt Stefan (Steve) Oancia, bomb-aimer to Ken Brown, Sgts "Doc" Sutherland and Harry O'Brien, Les Knight's gunners, F/S Ken Brown, F/S Harvey Weeks, rear gunner to Les Munro, W/O John Thrasher, Rice's bomb-aimer, F/S George Deering, Gibson's front gunner, Sgt Bill Radcliffe, flight engineer to Les Munro, F/S Don MacLean, navigator in Joe McCarthy's crew, F/L Joe McCarthy himself, and F/S Grant MacDonald, Ken Brown's rear gunner. Front row from the left are W/O Percy Pigeon, Munro's wireless operator, P/O "Terry" Taerum, Gibson's navigator, F/O Danny Walker Shannon's navigator, W/O Chester Gowrie, sparks in Rice's crew and F/O Dave Rodger, McCarthy's rear gunner. Some of the above were in the RAF, while others were RCAF. A number of those in the latter category were not Canadians by birth, Americans Joe McCarthy and Dave Rodger, for example, having joined the RCAF before American came into the war. George Deering was born in Ireland.

There were just two Kiwi founder members of 617 Squadron, F/L Les Munro, seen here on the right, and F/O Len Chambers, who served as wireless operator in "Mick" Martin's crew. Munro was a farmer before enlisting, and served with 97 Squadron before his posting to 617. Chambers was a carpenter back home and joined up in 1940. He completed a tour of 31 operations with 75(NZ) Squadron, and was at 26 O.T.U. when posted to 617 Squadron on the 7th of April.

Wing Commander George Holden was posted to 617 Squadron as commanding officer elect on the 2nd of July 1943. His operational career to this point had been spent in 4 Group, beginning with 78 Squadron at Dishforth, where he served for a time under the now Air Commodore "Charles" Whitworth. He took part in the first SAS operation, which involved the parachuting of a special force, known as X-Troop, No 11 SAS Battalion, into the Foggia region of Italy to destroy an aqueduct. The Whitley element was led by W/C James Tait, another future commanding officer of 617 Squadron. In the event, the operation failed. After twenty operations with 78 Squadron, Holden joined 35 Squadron, which was introducing the Halifax into operational service. He flew a further twelve operations, including a daylight attack on the German cruiser *Scharnhorst* in July 1941, before being screened to become an instructor. During this period he was put in charge of 405 RCAF Squadron's Conversion Flight, where Johnny Fauquier was the commanding officer, and he too would ultimately take the helm at 617. Holden took part in the second and third thousand bomber raids against Essen and Bremen in June 1942, and was then posted to 158 Squadron's Conversion Flight. In October 1942 he was given command of 102 Squadron, when his predecessor was killed in a freak accident. He was rested again in April 1943 with a total of 45 operations to his credit, and assumed command of 617 Squadron on Gibson's departure on the 3rd of August.

Among the first new recruits posted in to 617 Squadron to fill the gaps created by Operation *Chastise*'s heavy losses was S/L Ralf Allsebrook. He was a veteran of the Hampden days, having completed a first tour with 49 Squadron at Scampton, which included a ditching on the way home from Mannheim in February 1942. He was awarded the DFC in April of that year, and after a period of screening returned to 49 Squadron in January 1943 to begin a second tour. He was by then a flight lieutenant, but he came to 617 Squadron as an acting squadron leader and flight commander elect. This photograph was taken in April 1943 at Fiskerton, and shows Allsebrook with his crew standing in front of their 49 Squadron Lancaster ED597 EA-B. L – R F/O Grant, wireless operator, F/S Lulham, bomb-aimer, Allsebrook, P/O Botting, navigator, F/S Hitchen, rear gunner, Sgt Jones, mid-upper gunner and F/S Moore, flight engineer.

Another picture of Allsebrook and crew probably taken at the same time as previous one. Here five members of ground crew join the gathering, and P/O Botting is the one smiling from the frame of the door.

A reconnaissance photograph of the Möhne Dam taken during preparations for Operation *Chastise* shows its graceful curve, the booms supporting the torpedo nets and the original power station nestling in the shadow of the giant wall. The Möhne reservoir lies twenty-five miles east of Dortmund, in a beautiful hilly region a few miles beyond the industrial Ruhr and south of the small town of Soest. The huge dam, at the time the largest in Europe, took four years to construct and was completed in 1913. It stands at the north-western corner of the reservoir, a magnificent arc of concrete and masonry stretching 850 yards across the valley, with its twenty-five-foot wide crest and roadway standing 120 feet above the bedrock to which the structure is anchored. At its base the dam is more than a hundred feet thick, and after each year's spring rains its gravity and form alone hold in check around 140 million tons of water. Although never seriously considered by the German authorities to be a potential target, the dam face was protected by the two substantial torpedo nets that reached the lakebed. A matter of days before the war broke out a Ruhr city official had written to the authorities raising the matter of protection for the dams in the event of attack from the air, and he had at first been politely humoured. After about three years of correspondence, however, and a number of testy responses to the constant nagging, a few 20mm flak pieces were sent to the Möhne in the hope that that would put an end to the matter.

The morning after the night before. An RAF reconnaissance Spitfire cruises over the Möhne Reservoir on Monday morning the 17th of May 1943 to photograph the results of Operation *Chastise*. Water still flows gently through the clearly visible breach, while the emerging sandbanks demonstrate the massive volume of water that has already drained away in a flood wave that took the lives of many hundreds of people. More than a third of the total casualties were eastern European slave workers, whose wooden barrack accommodation lay in the path of the maelstrom. Just visible in the sandbank at the southern extremity of the dam is a crater, believed to be that caused by Martin's bomb after it veered off course. There is also faint evidence of a disturbance in the lake bed a few yards short of and a little to the north of the southern sluice tower, just where Gibson's bomb exploded. This is best viewed through a magnifying glass. The power station has completely disappeared. It was destroyed by Hopgood's bomb, which leapt over the wall and detonated on contact with it, and the debris was then swept away a few minutes later by the torrent of water resulting from Maltby's bomb.

An aerial reconnaissance photo of the Eder Dam. In contrast to the situation at the Möhne, no one believed the Eder Dam required a defence. It lies in equally beautiful but more rugged terrain some sixty miles to the south-east of the Möhne, and is enfolded in high hills providing natural protection. The Eder was completed in 1914, and although only half the span of the Möhne, it stands twenty-five feet higher, with a twenty foot wide crest and 119 foot base. The Eder reservoir was the largest in Germany and at its fullest contains two hundred million tons of water.

The Eder Dam after 617 Squadron's visit on the morning of Monday 17th of May 1943. The breach from a perfect delivery by Les Knight was narrower than that at the Möhne, but deeper, and this allowed a higher flood wave to develop and wreake havoc in the countryside beyond.

Bill Astell concentrates on the job of flying the Lancaster. Gibson, himself, commented on the strength required to manhandle the heavy bomber, particularly at low level, where "ground effects" increased the level of turbulence. Operation *Chastise* would ask many questions of the pilots, who would be at under 100 feet for most of the roughly six hours duration of the raid.

P/O Floyd Wile was the navigator, and one of three Canadians in Astell's crew. He was born in Nova Scotia in April 1919 as the fifth of seven children. Following high school he worked on the land as a farm hand and in the lumber industry. He had shown an interest in radio during his youth, and actually studied the subject for a year at technical school. He was also keen on sporting activities, particularly skiing, skating and swimming. Before enlisting in the RCAF he joined a local army unit in Yarmouth, Nova Scotia, but resigned after a month. At 5 Initial Training School he was noted as being slow thinking, hard working, the plodder type, while at No 8 Air Observer School he was described as average, with the comment, "in no respect has he shown much aptitude for work." Another report described him as a quiet lad, and backward through lack of experience in mixing. Three months later, however, his commanding officer at No 9 Bombing and Gunnery School called him outstanding and a brilliant trainee, who was very popular and had good self-control. Despite this he passed out of No 2 Air Navigation School with a "not outstanding, average NCO material" tag, but was commissioned as a Pilot Officer before leaving Wigsley in December 1942.

A view from the cockpit of a Lancaster during training for Operation *Chastise*. The snapshot was taken in April by Sgt Abram Garshowitz, wireless operator to F/L Bill Astell.

A view from the astrodome. Garshowitz captures another Lancaster in his lens, and it can be clearly recognised as a standard production model.

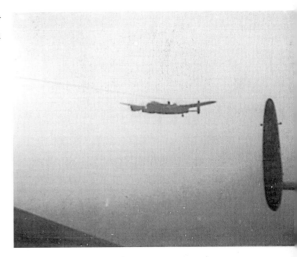

An impressive view of ED817 pictured during the summer of 1943. This was the second prototype Dams Lancaster, and the hole where the mid-upper turret would normally have been seems to be quite roughly patched up. Here coded AJ-C it later became AJ-X, and was eventually sent to 46 Maintenance Unit.

Flight engineer Sgt Jock Kinnear keeps watch through the right hand side of the glass house. Beyond him beneath the control panel is the tunnel access to the bomb-aimer's compartment and the front turret. Kinnear did not become involved with Astell and the others until they had already carried out four operations with 57 Squadron. He was born in Fife Scotland in November 1921, and grew up to be a likeable, carefree young man who was mad about flying. He worked as a mechanic until he was old enough to enlist, and this he did in 1939. He was at 1654CU at the same time as the other members of his future crew, but does not appear to have arrived at 57 Squadron until later. He flew his first operations with the crew against Hamburg on the night of the 3/4th of March 1943 and Essen two nights later.

The photographer caught in his own lens. Abram Garshowitz peers through the cockpit blister. He was born in Hamilton, Ontario, in December 1920. Known within his family as Albert, he was the ninth of twelve children, and went to school locally. Afterwards he worked in the family business selling new and used furniture. His close friend, Frank Garbas, with whom Garshowitz played semi-pro American football with the Eastwood Lions before enlisting in the RCAF, was also a member of Astell's crew.

A view of the Ennerpe Dam. There is some doubt as to whether Townsend attacked this dam or the one at the nearby Bever Reservoir. There is evidence to support both viewpoints, but as AJ-O's bomb failed to reach the dam wall and there was no damage, it is unlikely that a definitive conclusion will ever be reached. The Ennerpe was one of the subsidiary targets along with the Diemel and Lister Dams, which were to be attacked only when the Möhne, Eder and Sorpe had been confirmed as destroyed.

The dry side of the Lister Dam, which has only one tower, and this would have made it difficult to attack with the sighting method employed at the Möhne and Eder.

A shot of the Lister Dam from the reservoir side showing the pronounced curve of the masonry structure.

The remains of the little church in the village of Himmelpforten (Gates of Heaven), which was directly in the path of the flood wave resulting from the destruction of the Möhne Dam. There had been a religious building on this site for 700 years, beginning with a convent. The church, called Porta Coeli, which means gates of heaven in Latin, was famous for its valuable statues, carvings and other articles. Paster Berkenkopf had been the clergyman for the villages of Himmelpforten and Niederense for thirty years, and apparently had an arrangement with his parishioners, that, in the event of a threat to the Dam, he would ring the church bell as a warning. It is said that he was still tugging on the bell rope as the church and the villages were swept away down the valley. When the flood waters had subsided there was little evidence to show that a church had ever existed on that spot. Paster Berkenkopf's body was nowhere to be found, and the local authorities declared it pointless to conduct a search. The villagers, however, were determined to find him, and dug their way into the cellar with bare hands and whatever tools they could find. Eventually their labours were rewarded, and the pastors mortal remains were found under the rubble. A small piece of masonry was erected using original materials, and a plaque bears the sad story of the events of the 17th of May 1943.

A close-up post-raid shot of Gibson's Dams Lancaster ED932, showing the additional cable cutters on the leading edges considered necessary for ultra low flying, and the thin VHF whip aerial protruding diagonally from the starboard lower fuselage.

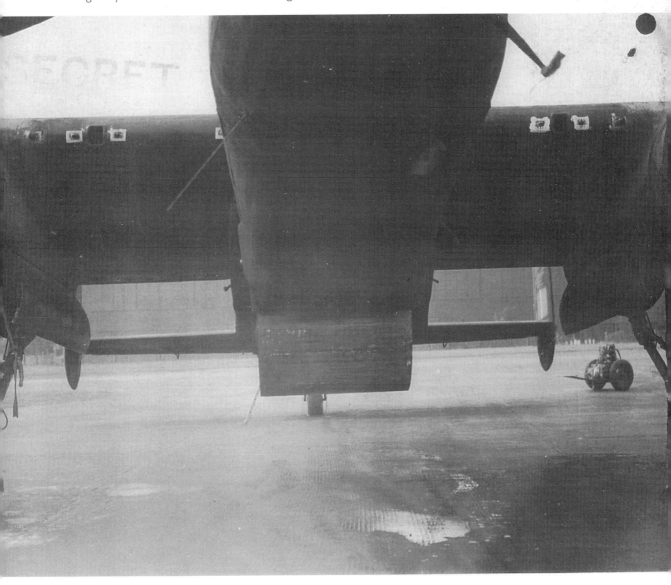

ED932 on what looks like a misty morning at Scampton. This picture was taken during the summer of 1943, and shows the retaining arms clamping the *Upkeep*, and the drive belt attached to the hydraulic motor inside the fuselage that imparted backspin of 500 rpm prior to release. ED932 was one of two type 464 Lancasters to have the direction of spin reversed in an attempt to increase the range of *Upkeep* for employment on land against viaducts. In the event the trials produced inconsistent results, and *Upkeep* was never used in anger again.

"Mickey" Martin and Bob Hay in good humour at Scampton post *Chastise*. The Lancaster in the background is a standard model.

Out with the old, in with the new. Gibson poses with his successor, George Holden, and his Dams crew and ground crew in front of ED932 at Scampton on the 2nd of August 1943, Gibson's last day as commanding officer of 617 Squadron. Air crew members from L – R are Taerum, Deering, Trevor-Roper, Hutchison, Gibson, Holden, Pulford and Spafford. The man between Gibson and Holden is Cpl Derek Wood, a fitter. Tragically, not one of these airmen would survive the war. Holden, Deering, Taerum, Spafford and Hutchison would all die at Nordhorn on the way to the Dortmund-Ems Canal on the 16th of September. Pulford was to lose his life in a crash on the South Downs near Chichester on the 13th of February 1944, as S/L Bill Suggitt attempted to get back to Woodhall Spa after landing at Ford following an attack on the Antheor Viaduct. Richard Trevor-Roper left 617 Squadron, and died in the rear turret of a Pathfinder Lancaster from 97 Squadron during the catastrophic Nuremberg operation of the 30/31st of March 1944. Gibson failed to return from Mönchengladbach on the 19/20th of September 1944.

DV402 stands on a small Sardinian landing strip on the 13th of February 1944 as local airfield workers get a close up look at an example of the RAF's pride and joy. During the course of an attack on the Antheor Viaduct on France's Riviera coast, Martin's Lancaster was hit by flak. A piece of shrapnel killed F/L Bob Hay, the squadron bombing leader, whose remains are buried on the island. The exit hole in the starboard side of the bomb-aimer's compartment provides evidence of the encounter. Flight engineer Ivan Whittaker was also wounded, although not seriously. This was the squadron's third gallant failure against the target, which was an important link in the communications chain between France and Italy. The Lancaster was repaired and returned to service with 617 Squadron, and survived the war.

F/L Bill Astell was earmarked to be Young's deputy as A Flight commander at 617 Squadron. He was born in 1920 at Peover in Cheshire to an upper class family, which, by the thirties was resident in Chapel-en-le-Frith on the edge of the Peak District of Derbyshire. His father, Godfrey, was the managing director of J & N Philips, a textile company, which he ran from its main site in Church Street, Manchester. The family's affluence enabled Bill to travel extensively overseas to broaden his education and experience, and in 1936, at the age of sixteen, he sailed to Canada to visit relatives. He also took a trip to the White Sea in a trawler. He spent the end of 1937, most of 1938 and the first half of 1939 in Germany and France, and on his return to England he joined the RAF Air Reserve. He was posted for duty in Malta, but before he had an opportunity to get into the war, he was struck down by typhoid, and forced to spend time first in hospital and then convalescing. He finally joined 148 Squadron at Kabrit in Egypt in May 1941 and began operations as a Wellington pilot, attacking ports and landing grounds. A crash on the 30th of November left him with injuries, and he remained in hospital until February 1942. He returned to duty with 148 Squadron and a new crew in

March, and then on the last night of May he failed to return from an operation. Five days later he walked in to report crash-landing after being attacked by an enemy fighter over the target. He spent a few days in hospital in Tobruk, before being sent home via America, arriving back in England aboard the *Queen Mary* in September. He was posted to Wigsley in Nottinghamshire, one of 5 Group's training stations, and also spent time at Hullavington and Fulbeck. Now in the rank of Flight Lieutenant he was posted to 57 Squadron at Scampton on the 25th of January 1943 to undertake a second tour, this time on Lancasters, and it was here that he acquired his new crew. All who knew Astell, particularly those of the fairer sex, would testify to his open, friendly, charming nature, which made him immensely likeable.

W/C George Holden joined 78 Squadron at Dishforth in September 1940 after completing his training. After completing twenty operations he joined 35 Squadron at Linton-on-Ouse in February 1941. 35 Squadron had been reformed at Boscombe Down in November 1940 to introduce the Halifax into operational service, and was attracting the leading bomber pilots in 4 Group. The Halifax suffered many teething problems, and the demand for modifications ensured only a trickle of new aircraft from the factories. As a result, following its operational baptism in March, the type operated only intermittently and in very small numbers for some time. Holden flew his first Halifax sortie against Duisburg on the 11/12th of June, and over the ensuing five weeks managed ten more. Holden concluded his tour on a total of thirty-two operations, and was posted to the Heavy Conversion Flight at Linton-on-Ouse on the 18th of August. Here he remained until December, when he was detached to Upavon, before progressing to Marston Moor, Leeming and Pocklington progressively in the role of instructor. At Pocklington, and now in the rank of Squadron Leader, he was put in charge of the Conversion Flight of 405 Squadron, a Canadian unit commanded by W/C Johnny Fauquier. While there, Holden flew on the second thousand bomber raid against Essen on the 1/2nd of June 1942, and the third and final one on Bremen on the 25/26th, his thirty-third and thirty-fourth sorties. In July he was posted to 158 Squadron's Conversion Flight at East Moor, where he remained until the 25th of October. In the early hours of the previous day, 102 Squadron's commanding officer, W/C Bintley, had been killed in a freak accident on the runway at Holme-on-Spalding-Moor on return from Genoa, when another Halifax had crushed his cockpit on landing. Holden was posted in as his replacement on the 25th, and began a successful period of command, during which he operated a further eleven times, bringing his tally to forty-five. In this photo Holden is entertaining the children of the station intelligence officer.

Basil Feneron flew on Operation *Chastise* as Ken Brown's flight engineer. He joined the RAF in 1940, and as a sergeant was posted along with the other members of Brown's crew to begin his first tour with 44 (Rhodesia) Squadron on the 5th of February 1943. The crew was selected to be founder members to 617 Squadron, and moved to Scampton on the 25th of March. Feneron was commissioned in January 1944, and after exactly one year at 617 Squadron was posted to 1654 Conversion Unit for instructional duties. He continued to serve on various stations until his release in April 1946.

George Chalmers joined the RAF in 1938 and was a wireless operator with 10 Squadron at Dishforth when war broke out on the 3rd of September 1939. This 4 Group squadron was operating its Whitleys on leafleting sorties before the war was a week old. When 7 Squadron was reformed in 3 Group at Leeming in August 1940 to bring the new four-engine Stirling to operational service, Chalmers was posted from 10 Squadron to join it. The same thing happened again in November, when 7 Squadron moved out of Leeming and 35 Squadron moved in from Boscombe Down, where it had reformed two weeks earlier to bring the Halifax to operational status. This meant a return to 4 Group for Chalmers, and he remained on operations until being screened in February 1942. On the 6th of April 1943 he was posted to 5 Group to join 617 Squadron, by which time he had more than forty sorties to his credit. He joined the crew of F/S Bill Townsend, who had arrived from 49 Squadron in March. Chalmer's DFM was gazetted on the 28th of May 1943, and he was commissioned a month later. His DFC awarded in October 1944 recognised sixty-five operations. He retired from the RAF in 1954.

Dudley Heal was a crewmate of Basil Feneron in the crew of Ken Brown, and occupied the navigator's seat for the attack on the Sorpe Dam during Operation *Chastise*. He joined the RAF in 1940 and arrived at 44 (Rhodesia) Squadron in February 1943. The crew flew six operations before being posted to Scampton as founder members of 617 Squadron on the 25th of March. The award of the DFM was gazetted on the 18th of May. Heal left 617 Squadron for 29 Operational Training Unit after one year, and spent the final months of the war with 214 Squadron, and was released from the RAF in March 1946.

Henry Maudslay was born in Royal Leamington Spa, Warwickshire in July 1921, and four years later the family moved to the village of Sherbourne, a few miles to the southwest of Warwick. His parents were Reginald, who died in 1934, and Susan, and he had a sister, Margaret, who was eleven years his senior. The Maudslay family was connected with both the Standard Motor Company and the Maudslay Motor Company. Henry was sent to preparatory school in Gloucestershire, and attended Eton College from 1935 to 1940. Here he excelled as an athlete, both as a miler and as an oarsman, and his prowess was recognized in his election as Captain of Boats and Captain of Athletics during his final year. During this period, in 1937, the family moved to Foxhill Manor, an imposing house at Willersey in Worcestershire. Having volunteered for the RAF, he was called up in July 1940, and after beginning elementary flying training in Yorkshire and Shropshire, he was posted to Canada under the Commonwealth Air Training Plan. He returned to the UK in February 1941, and after training on Hampdens at 25 O.T.U., he was posted to 44 Squadron at Waddington as a Pilot Officer in May. From then until early November he flew a total of twenty-nine operations, before being detached to

Boscombe Down for Lancaster training. This period of his service is difficult to establish, but it seems that he was also detached to Rolls-Royce at Derby from the 7th to the 10th of January 1942. He returned to 44 Squadron Conversion Flight in January as an instructor, and was promoted to Flying Officer on the 29th, the day before his DFC was gazetted. He seems to have been at Boscombe Down again from the 9th to the 15th of February in some capacity connected with the Lancaster. He carried out no further operational sorties until the first one thousand-bomber raid on Cologne on the night of the 30/31st of May. For this momentous occasion he flew the Conversion Flight's Manchester L7430, an aircraft with a reputation as a "hack". Two nights later he took another "hack", Manchester L7480, to Essen for the second of the thousand-bomber raids, and completed the hat trick by operating against Bremen in the third and final of these mammoth efforts on the 25/26th of June in Lancaster R5862. In July he was posted to 1654CU at Wigsley, where 5 Group crews were converted to Lancasters, and here he came into contact with a number of future 617 Squadron recruits as they passed through his hands. He requested a return to operational duties at the earliest opportunity, and was posted to 50 Squadron at Skellingthorpe in January 1943. He completed another thirteen operations from here as a Flight Lieutenant, before moving to Scampton and 617 Squadron as a Squadron Leader and B Flight commander.

Shannon was just twenty years old when he joined 106 Squadron at Coningsby in June 1942, although he looked much younger. His first operation was as second pilot to S/L John Wooldridge, officer commanding B Flight, on the occasion of the third and final thousand-bomber raid on the night of the 25/26th of June. Wooldridge was one of the great characters of Bomber Command, and a man who preferred to compose classical music and write plays rather than carouse his off duty nights away with his squadron colleagues. The target for Wooldridge and his young charge on this night in June 1942 was the city of Bremen in north-western Germany, which had been a regular destination for Bomber Command almost since strategic bombing began in the summer of 1940. 960 Bomber Command aircraft were dispatched, along with 102 from Coastal Command, the latter on the personal orders of Churchill, and a moderately effective operation ensued. The 5 Group effort at Bremen, amounting to 142 aircraft, was directed entirely at the city's Focke-Wulf aircraft factory, and although it was not destroyed, an assembly shop was wrecked and six other buildings were severely damaged. Gibson had been absent from the squadron when Shannon arrived, and had not yet undertaken a Lancaster operation. His first, against Wilhelmshaven on the night of the 8/9th of July, was flown with Shannon as second pilot. Unlike many, Shannon was not overawed by Gibson's personality, and an

unshakable bond formed between the two men. Shannon's next four operations were flown as second dickey, and these included the daylight raid by 5 Group on the distant port of Danzig on the 11th of July, when he again flew with Gibson. Shannon did not operate at all during August, and when he undertook his first sortie as captain, a gardening expedition on the 4/5th of September, it proved to be something of an anticlimax, after W/T failure forced him to return early. Towards the end of November he was recommended for the non-immediate award of the DFC in recognition of his operational career thus far. For whatever reason Shannon's crew, with the exception of his navigator Danny Walker, opted not to accompany him to 617 Squadron, but he would gather around him excellent replacements, including bomb-aimer Len Sumpter, a former guardsman, who was older than most, and had completed thirteen operations with 57 Squadron by the time of his posting to 617 Squadron at the start of April.

Mick Martin and Bill Townsend. Sgt Bill Townsend was born in Gloucestershire in January 1921, and was educated at Monmouth School, where he became head boy and captained the rugby football team. It had always been his intention to join the Indian Army, but his application was deferred initially because of over-subscription. He was eventually called up to join the Royal Artillery on his twentieth birthday, but he found life less satisfying than expected, and volunteered to transfer to the RAF for pilot training. His new life began on the 14th of May 1941, and during the course of the next thirteen months he progressed through various training units, overcoming a tendency towards airsickness in the process. His training was completed at 16 O.T.U. at Upper Heyford, from where he took part in his first operational sorties, the thousand bomber raids on Cologne and Essen. He was posted to 49 Squadron at Scampton on the 12th of June 1942, and spent his first few months on the Conversion Flight learning to fly Manchesters and Lancasters. He began operations with the squadron in September, and by the time he joined 617 Squadron on the 25th of March 1943, his tally stood at twenty-seven. His commission as a Pilot Officer was backdated to the 16th of

March, and his DFM was gazetted on the 14th of May. Just two weeks later his part in Operation *Chastise* was recognised with the award of the Conspicuous Gallantry Medal. Ordered to attack the Ennepe Dam Townsend delivered his *Upkeep*, but it seems to have fallen short. By the time he reached Holland on the way back dawn had broken, but he avoided the defences to reach Scampton safely as the last man home. He was posted from 617 Squadron at the start of October 1943, and undertook instructional duties until completing his wartime service in India with South-East Asia Command.

Geoff Rice stands with members of his crew. From L – R Sgt Ed Smith, flight engineer, Geoff Rice, Sgt Stephen (Sandy or Ginger) Burns, rear gunner and navigator Flying Officer Richard MacFarlane. The other crew members were bomb-aimer P/O John Thrasher, wireless operator Warrant Officer Bruce Gowrie and front/mid-upper gunner F/Sgt Tom Maynard. Rice was the sole survivor when his Lancaster was shot down over Belgium by Hauptman Kurt Fladrich following an aborted operation against the Fabrique National gun factory at Liege on the night of the 20/21st of December 1943. Rice evaded capture for five months before being betrayed, and spent the remainder of the war as a guest of the Reich until being liberated by Russian soldiers in April 1945.

Joe McCarthy and Dave Shannon pose in front of the main entrance to the Petwood Hotel at Woodhall Spa in Lincolnshire, home to the officers serving at the nearby bomber station. "Big" Joe hailed from New York State, and joined the RCAF in 1941 before America entered the war. He completed a full tour with 97 Squadron and was awarded the DFC. His part in Operation *Chastise*, during which he accurately attacked the Sorpe Dam, was rewarded with a DSO. At the time of his departure from 617 Squadron for instructional duties in July 1944 he was a flight commander and recipient of a Bar to his DFC. Joe McCarthy survived the war and right up to his death was fiercely proud of his time with 617 Squadron, and maintained that Operation *Chastise* had been successful and worthwhile.

The greatest bomber baron of them all. Air Chief Marshal Sir Arthur Harris led Bomber Command from the 22nd of February 1942 until the end of hostilities on the 8th of May 1945. He was an advocate of the theory expounded by the Italian General Douhet after the Great War, which predicted future wars would be fought predominantly with air power. He foresaw giant armadas of self-defending bombers overflying the battle front and targeting the economic foundations of the enemy, destroying both its will and capacity to continue the fight. Harris learned his trade as a squadron commander in the Middle-East in the twenties, and used his time to develop the theory and practice of bombing by day and by night. When the Second World War erupted Harris was Air-Officer-Commanding 5 Group, a job he held until becoming a deputy to Chief-of-the-Air-Staff Sir Charles Portal late in 1940. Following a diplomatic mission to the United States, during which he helped cement the relationship between the two

nations, he succeeded Sir Richard Peirse as C-in-C Bomber Command. When he took up the reins the command was at its lowest ebb, but he introduced new tactics, pushed for new aids to navigation and bombing accuracy, and fought the Command's corner against its many critics to save it from dissolution. To his men he was "Butch" or "Butcher", which, in the black humour of the day, reflected what they saw as his willingness to send them to their death. They were, never the less, fiercely proud to serve under him, and to this day those who live on defend his policies and actions against and who would denounce him. Shabbily treated after the war, Harris was the only commander in the field not to be publicly recognised by Churchill, and those who served under him in Bomber Command were denied even the consolation of a campaign medal.

Air-Vice-Marshal Sir Ralph Cochrane was the Group commander to whom Harris gave the task of breaking the dams. He had been in post as A-O-C 5 Group for less than three weeks, and knew of Gibson only through Harris. Born in 1895 as the youngest son of the 1st Baron Cochrane of Cults, the Honourable Ralph Cochrane joined the Royal Navy in 1912, and transferred to the RAF in 1918. He served extensively in the Middle-East during the early twenties, for a period as a flight commander under Harris, and it was at this time that the two men forged a respect for and understanding of each other that would prove fruitful during the current conflict. Among his appointments in the thirties were spells as the first Chief of the Air Staff Royal New Zealand Air Force from the 1st of April 1937, and Air Aide-de-Camp to King George VI from September to December 1939. In October 1940 he became Director of Flying Training, a position he held until becoming A-O-C 3 Group in September 1942. Cochrane would consider any idea that might improve the cutting edge of his group, and this willingness to experiment led to 5 Group's independence from the spring of 1944. His notoriously strained relationship with Pathfinder chief AVM Bennett is legendary. Both were brilliant men, with completely opposite ideas on target marking, and both achieved highly successful results. However, Cochrane's long standing relationship with Harris gave him the edge, and generally he came out on top.

W/C G L Cheshire became a legend in Bomber Command, and was equally revered for his post war activities. Until joining 617 Squadron in November 1943 he had been a 4 Group man to the core. He had begun his operational career as a Flying Officer flying Whitleys with 102 Squadron in June 1940, where he was a contemporary of the late "Dinghy" Young. On the 12/13th of November he brought a massively damaged aircraft safely back from Germany, and received an immediate award of the DSO, thus giving an insight into the character that would make him one of the most famous warriors in Bomber Command. With the advent of the Halifax, Cheshire was posted to 35 Squadron in January 1941, to join the likes of Tait and Holden, and was awarded the DFC in March. In early May, while the Halifaxes were grounded for essential modifications to be carried out, he landed a posting to the Atlantic Ferry Organisation and departed for Canada. A surplus of pilots caused him to kick his heels, and he took the opportunity to visit New York. Here he met the retired actress Constance Binney, whom he married in July. He returned alone to the UK soon afterwards to rejoin 35 Squadron, and set about persuading the Foreign Office to allow Constance to join him. This she did in October, and they set up home in a flat in Harrogate. Promotion to Flight Lieutenant had come in June, and at the conclusion of his second tour in February 1942 he was posted as an instructor to 1652HCU at Marston Moor. During this time he was writing his book, Bomber Pilot, which he had finished before he participated in all three of the thousand bomber raids in May and June. He returned to a front line operational squadron in August 1942 as a Wing Commander, when given command of 76 Squadron, the unit in which his brother Christopher had served as a pilot until being shot down on his way to Berlin a year earlier. Christopher had survived, and was on extended leave in a PoW camp. Cheshire remained at 76 Squadron until April 1943, and at the conclusion of this, his third tour, he was promoted to Group Captain and posted as station commander to Marston Moor, a 4 Group training station. Here he had a converted railway carriage transported onto the site, where he lived with Constance. Although throwing himself into his new job, Cheshire was never really happy at being away from the operational scene, and when offered the post at 617 Squadron, he eagerly accepted it, even though it meant having to revert to the rank of Wing Commander. At the conclusion of his time with 617 Squadron in July 1944 he was awarded the Victoria Cross in recognition of one hundred operations.

Target photograph of the Gnome & Rhone aero engine factory at Limoges, attacked by 617 Squadron on the night of the 8/9th of February 1944. Cheshire made three runs across the target at low level to warn the workers, and give them time to vacate the factory. On his fourth run he dropped his incendiaries into the centre of the roof from under a hundred feet, and Martin backed up with his spot fires and incendiaries some four minutes later. Five crews waiting above at 8,000 to 10,000 feet were carrying 12,000 pounders, Shannon, Clayton, Brown, Ross and Willsher, and four of these were direct hits, while Willsher's undershot by about 150 yards. The remaining five crews carried eleven 1,000 pounders each, and most of these fell across the target, although Wilson reported his bombs to have fallen at least fifty yards to the left after the plug on the control switch was found to be pulled out. The operation was an outstanding success, and the dramatic events were captured on cine-film. A photograph of Cheshire's markers cascading onto the factory was released to the press, and the actual footage has found its way into many documentary films since. Reconnaissance photographs showed immense damage to the target, with nine medium bay sized workshops and a large multi-bay building all suffering heavily. Twenty-one out of forty-eight bays were destroyed, and a further twenty were badly damaged. Other buildings in the target area were also affected, and even the bays remaining intact had sustained internal damage from blast. This aiming point photo flash exposure was taken from 10,400 feet at 00.06 hours by Lieutenant Nick Knilans in Lancaster KC-R, ME561. This aircraft went on to complete all three operations against the *Tirpitz*, but crashed in Lincolnshire on return from Pölitz in the early hours of the 22nd of December 1944 while in the hands of F/O Joplin, as a result of which two crew members lost their lives.

As previous page, but taken from KC-M, DV394, being flown on this night by Dams veteran Ken Brown. This Lancaster was shot down by a night fighter during an operation to Munich on the night of the 24/25th of April 1944 while being flown by F/L Cooper and his crew. The bomb-aimer was killed, but the others fell into enemy hands.

A post raid reconnaissance photograph shows the destruction at Limoges following the previously-mentioned operation by 617 Squadron.

Just one operation involved 617 Squadron during May, and even then it was only the Mosquito crews who were called upon. It was mounted on the 3rd, when the target for that night for 346 Lancasters of 1 and 5 Groups was the Panzer training camp and motor transport depot at Mailly-le-Camp in France. The plan was for 617 Squadron Mosquitos to mark two aiming points, one for each Group, before handing the target over to the master bomber. Cheshire was to act as marker leader, while W/C Deane of 83 Squadron was the overall controller. Initially all went to plan, but a communications problem arose, when a commercial radio station jammed the VHF frequencies in use. A few crews heard the call to bomb, and did so, but for most the instructions were swamped by the interference. The 1 Group crews in particular were forced to wait in the target area, and they became increasingly agitated as the bright moonlight aided the enemy night fighters. As burning aircraft were seen to fall all around, some 1 Group crews succumbed to their anxiety and frustration, and in a rare breakdown of R/T discipline let fly with comments of an uncomplimentary nature, many of which were intended for and, indeed, heard by Deane. Despite the confusion the operation was a major success, which destroyed 80% of the camp's buildings, and 102 vehicles, of which thirty-seven were tanks, while over two hundred men were killed. Forty-two Lancasters failed to return, two thirds of them from 1 Group. This photo shows the target under attack.

A photo-reconnaissance aircraft captures the results of the previous night's effort against the site at Mailly, and the devastation is clearly evident.

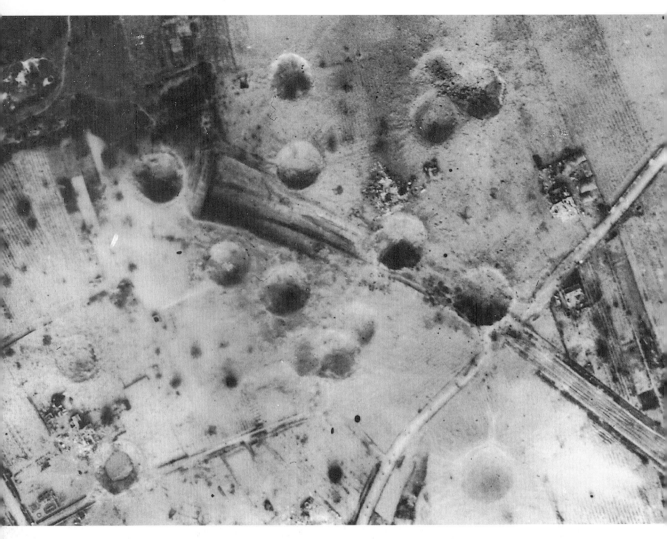

Immediately following the Normandy landings on D-Day, Bomber Command attacked communications targets in France to prevent the enemy from bringing up reinforcements. 617 Squadron was assigned to the Saumur railway tunnel on the 8th of June, and employed for the very first time the new Barnes Wallis designed 12,000lb *Tallboy* deep penetration or "earthquake" bomb. Photographic reconnaissance after the raid showed an 85-foot diameter crater in the roof of the tunnel, and a total of seventeen others of varying dimensions within 220 yards of the southern entrance. The tracks were cut around one hundred yards from this entrance, while a near miss on a road/rail intersection some distance away had cut all tracks and damaged the road. There was also a large crater blocking a road 180 yards east of the northern entrance. The evidence pointed to an entirely successful operation, and it seemed at least, that the tracks were still blocked up to two months after the operation. However, documentation surfaced after the war to suggest that the tunnel had been quickly returned to use by the Germans, but that the appearance of devastation was allowed to remain to give a false impression and discourage a further attack. This operation had been carried out without adequate training, and in due course accuracy would improve dramatically.

Tallboy was a twenty-one foot long aerodynamically and ballistically perfect weapon, engineered to a very high standard. It was the next step in Wallis's use of shock wave technology to destroy otherwise impregnable structures. The shark-like projectile had to withstand an impact velocity, if dropped from its optimum height of 18,000 feet, of 750 m.p.h., after falling for thirty-seven seconds. In order to achieve this without breaking up, it boasted a case thickness near its nose of more than four inches, and carried a charge weight of 5,200lbs of Torpex. The depth of penetration into the earth depended upon the fuse delay time from 0.025 seconds upwards. At deepest penetration it was estimated to be capable of displacing one million cubic feet of earth, and creating a crater requiring five thousand tons of earth to refill it. An instantaneous detonation, on the other hand, would produce a crater twenty-five feet in depth, and more than eighty yards across. In time, this revolutionary weapon would prove to have a number of unanticipated abilities. The weapon seen falling in this dramatic shot has come from Don Cheney's KC-V "Dark Victor", and it is heading towards the V-Weapon storage site at Watten on the 19th of June 1944.

Views of *Tallboys* showing the offset fins that imparted a spin to the falling projectile. This prevented toppling and ensured that the weapon would with unerring precision towards the target.

| YEAR 1944 | | AIRCRAFT | | PILOT, OR | 2ND PILOT, PUPIL | DUTY |
MONTH	DATE	Type	No.	1ST PILOT	OR PASSENGER	(INCLUDING RESULTS AND REN
						TOTALS BROUGHT FO
JUNE	4	LANCASTER	JB139	SELF	P/O WELCH SGT. ROSHER F/S. POOL F/S. WAIT	AIR TEST
JUNE	5	LANCASTER	DV402	SELF	F/O KELL + CREW P/O WELCH F/S POOL F/S CURTIS F/S McROSTIE SGT ROSHER	SPECIAL OPERATIO TO ASSIST LANDIN IN NORTHERN FR "OPERATION TAXABLE
JUNE	8	LANCASTER	JB672	SELF	P/O WELCH F/S CURTIS F/S POOL F/O WAIT F/S McROSTIE SGT ROSHER	AIR TEST
JUNE	8	LANCASTER	JB139	SELF	P/O WELCH F/S CURTIS F/S POOL F/S McROSTIE F/S WAIT SGT ROSHER	OPS. SAUMUR T 1 × 14000 LBS. TAL N° 26 FIRST ATTACK USING TALL
JUNE	11	LANCASTER	JB139	SELF	P/O WELCH P/O CURTIS F/S POOL F/S WAIT F/S McROSTIE SGT ROSHER	AIR TEST
JUNE	12	LANCASTER	JB139	SELF	P/O WELCH F/S CURTIS F/S POOL F/S WAIT F/S McROSTIE SGT. ROSHER	AIR TEST

GRAND TOTAL [Cols. (1) to (10)]
719 Hrs. 30 Mins.

TOTALS CARRIED F

A page from Don Cheney's log book showing the special operation on D-Day Eve 5th of June and the attack on the Saumur Tunnel on the 8th. More than a thousand Bomber Command aircraft were in action on the night of the 5/6th of June, most of them to target coastal defences close to the landing beaches. 617 and 218 Squadrons were engaged in Operations *Taxable* and *Glimmer* respectively. The intention was to divert the enemy's attention away from the actual landing grounds along the Normandy coast, by making them believe the invasion was destined for the Pas-de-Calais, thus reinforcing an already long-held German conviction. No details of this highly secret operation were made available for entry into the Operations Record Book. Each 617 Squadron Lancaster carried two pilots, and up to twelve other crew members. Cheshire led the operation and the first of two sections

SUPREME HEADQUARTERS
ALLIED EXPEDITIONARY FORCE

Soldiers, Sailors and Airmen of the Allied Expeditionary Force!

You are about to embark upon the Great Crusade, toward which we have striven these many months. The eyes of the world are upon you. The hopes and prayers of liberty-loving people everywhere march with you. In company with our brave Allies and brothers-in-arms on other Fronts, you will bring about the destruction of the German war machine, the elimination of Nazi tyranny over the oppressed peoples of Europe, and security for ourselves in a free world.

Your task will not be an easy one. Your enemy is well trained, well equipped and battle-hardened. He will fight savagely.

But this is the year 1944! Much has happened since the Nazi triumphs of 1940-41. The United Nations have inflicted upon the Germans great defeats, in open battle, man-to-man. Our air offensive has seriously reduced their strength in the air and their capacity to wage war on the ground. Our Home Fronts have given us an overwhelming superiority in weapons and munitions of war, and placed at our disposal great reserves of trained fighting men. The tide has turned! The free men of the world are marching together to Victory!

I have full confidence in your courage, devotion to duty and skill in battle. We will accept nothing less than full Victory!

Good Luck! And let us all beseech the blessing of Almighty God upon this great and noble undertaking.

Dwight D. Eisenhower

as second pilot to Munro, while the McCarthy/Shannon combination headed the second section. In order to give the impression of a fleet of ships advancing at eight knots towards the French coast at Cap d'Antifer, sixty miles east of the Normandy beaches, eight 617 Squadron Lancasters had to fly line abreast two miles apart at 180 miles an hour dispensing Window at the rate of one bundle every five seconds. After heading for the French coast, all aircraft turned to port to complete an elliptical circuit lasting seven minutes. Each new circuit advanced the forward travel of the formation by one minute. The second section would take off later to be in place to relieve the first section after two hours. Each aircraft remained airborne for four and a half hours, two of which were spent windowing, and the crews flew their routines flawlessly, if unspectacularly.

A view of Scampton from above. This photo, taken from a 49 Squadron aircraft on the 3rd of October 1939, demonstrates the effectiveness of camouflage. The hedges have been painted onto the grass to deceive German reconnaissance aircraft. To the right of the buildings the arrow-straight A15 runs north to south past the main entrance and guardroom, and this was the spot at which Gibson's dog Nigger was run down by a car the day before Operation *Chastise* was launched.

A hero gives blood! Gibson shot to fame after the publicity surrounding Operation *Chastise* catapulted him into the public eye. Following his return from a lecture tour in America he dabbled in politics and set an example by donating blood. It is not known whether anyone was transfused with the VC's red stuff.

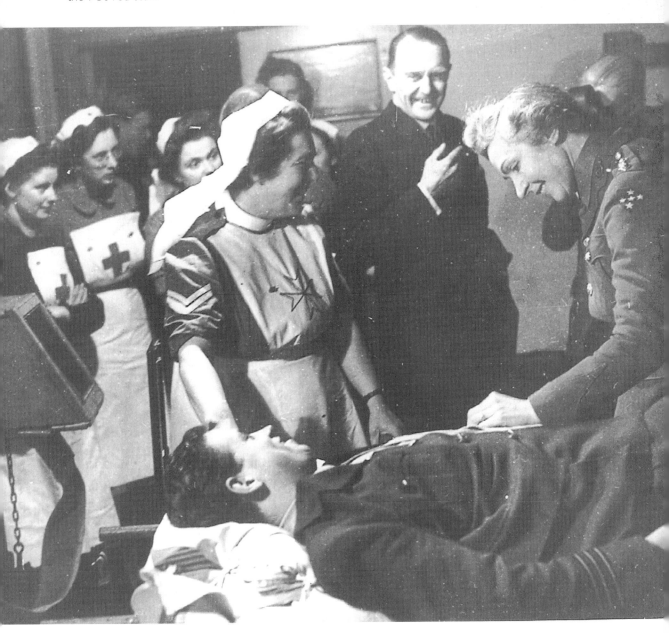

Early in 1944 Gibson was persuaded to offer himself for selection as the Conservative parliamentary candidate for Macclesfield in Cheshire. There was some opposition to his nomination, and ultimately he decided not to pursue the matter. Here he is seen outside the town hall in Macclesfield with local Tories.

On his way to give blood Gibson inspects a guard of honour of Air Training Corps cadets.

A series of reconnaissance photographs show the damage inflicted on the V-Weapon storage site at Wizernes in France. On the 24th of June 1944 Cheshire led the squadron in an operation against this target involving sixteen Lancasters and two Mosquitos. *Tallboys* rained down from either side of 17,000 feet, and bomb bursts were observed all around the target, on the railway line and near the mouth of the tunnel. Bill Reid saw one *Tallboy* penetrate the roof, and appear to burst inside causing an eruption but no smoke. A number of very near misses were claimed, and, as Barnes Wallis was to assert, a near miss with an earthquake bomb was probably more effective than a direct hit, and would destroy a concrete structure by its shock wave effect. On the 17th of July W/C Tait climbed into the

Mustang to lead the squadron for the first time in a return to Wizernes. Over the next sixteen minutes the *Tallboys* were delivered onto the target, and bomb bursts were seen all around the structure. One direct hit on the concrete dome was claimed by Bob Knights, but this proved to be an error, as photo reconnaissance revealed that no direct hits had been scored. There were, however, two large craters in an adjoining quarry, which caused a minor landslide, and evidence of other hits on the railway track and the tunnel entrance. It was a very successful operation, which sealed once and for all the fate of the site, although this was not at the time appreciated, and Harris would launch further operations against it.

'La Coupole' close up of the domed roof at Wizernes showing damage by 617 Squadron. The massive concrete dome was shifted out of alignment by close hits from Tallyboys. Wizernes was a proposed V-2 Rocket assembly and launch site constructed on a former limestone quarry.

Another angle showing damage by 617 Squadron on the Wizernes V weapons site. Part of the hillside collapsed causing tunnel blockage and further damage to the site, which was eventually abandoned.

The Kembs Barrage stands astride the Rhine at the junction of Germany, Switzerland and France, and on the very outskirts of the Swiss city of Basle. On the 7th of October thirteen 617 Squadron crews were briefed for a daylight attack on the structure. Immediately north of Basle the river divides into two branches in the shape of the letter Y running roughly northwest to southeast, and the dam-like objective, with its steelwork superstructure, stretched across the right-hand or eastern branch a matter of a few hundred metres north of the point of divide. The plan called for a high section of seven Lancasters to deliver their *Tallboys* first, and then for the remaining six aircraft to go in in pairs at around 600 feet with their *Tallboys* fused for a delay of thirty minutes. Three squadrons of Mustangs were on hand to provide air cover and deal with the flak positions. Two of the low section were hit by the fierce ground fire, and Kit Howard and his crew died in the resulting crash in a nearby wood. Wyness managed to carry out a controlled ditching in the Rhine, and three of his crew scrambled along the wing and reached the French bank. They were never seen again and are assumed to have been murdered. Wyness and three others made for the Swiss bank in the dinghy, but were apprehended and murdered by local Nazi Party officials. Tait's bomb was later seen to explode and create a breach in the barrage.

A target photograph of the Kembs Barrage during the attack showing bomb bursts all around. The explosion at the right hand end of the barrage could be that from Jimmy Castagnola's *Tallboy*. On landing he claimed a direct hit between piers 1 and 2, the approximate location of Tait's successful drop.

Phil Martin in his "office" above the motif of St George and the Dragon. F/O Phil Martin was another Australian who had joined 61 Squadron after a spell flying Wellingtons at 17 O.T.U., at Silverstone during December 1943 and January 1944, while the Berlin campaign was at its height. He was introduced to four engines via Stirlings at 1660CU at Swinderby, before spending twelve days learning to fly the Lancaster at 5 LFS Syerston. His first operation with 61 Squadron was as a second pilot on the 5 Group raid against Brunswick led by the 617 Squadron Mosquitos on the 22/23rd of April. With this one in the bag he completed another thirty sorties, finishing with a small-scale daylight attack by the Group on oil storage installations at La Pallice on the 19th of August.

F/O Phil Martin and crew standing on the wing of their Lancaster at Woodhall Spa.

Y/617. S/LDR. WYNESS. KEGOSTROV.

The wreckage of ME559 KC-Y lies at Kegostrov awaiting modification. It was one of six Lancasters left behind in Russia after running out of fuel while searching for Yagodnik, the staging post for the first *Tirpitz* operation in the Archangel region of Russia. Of these four were from 9 Squadron, while the two 617 Squadron aircraft belonged to Ross and Wyness. They were abandoned either because they were deemed to be beyond repair, or after having been cannibalised to keep the others airworthy. Russian Air Force personnel inspected them, and decided, that the two least damaged could be returned to flying condition. They were dismantled and transported to Kegostrov for repair and modification by the Air Force of the White Sea, which was to use them for unarmed marine patrols. The armament was removed, and the rear turret faired-over, while a Mk III Halifax style perspex nose was added, along with larger side windows for better observation. The RAF colour scheme was retained, but red stars outlined in black replaced the roundels. The Lancaster pictured was that flown to Russia by S/L Wyness, which now, with Russian owners, became 01, its new identification painted large in white. It was allocated to the 16th Transport Flight for convoy escort, submarine detection and general reconnaissance flights, and as a result of its handling qualities and long range, it proved to be popular with its new owners. It survived the war, and its last known role was as an educational aid at the Russian Aviation Technical College. The original identity of the other restored Lancaster is not known, but it was written off in a crash at the end of the war.

Lancasters at Yagodnik taken from PD233. Those on the front rank belong to 9 Squadron. 617 Squadron Lancasters lined up astern as they wait for the right conditions to carry out Operation *Paravane*, the first of three attacks on the *Tirpitz* at its Norwegian moorings.

F/O Ian Ross's EE131 KC-B lies in a field near Molotov after coming down in the circumstances described previously. Ross's luck ran out during a daylight operation to U-Boot pens at Bergen in Norway on the 12th of January 1945. His Lancaster was seen by Freddie Watts to be trailing smoke as it was chased out to sea by two FW190 fighters. NF992 was clearly losing the fight with gravity, and the crippled Lancaster sank lower and lower over the cold ocean. Watts instinctively dived in pursuit of the pursuers, at the same time seeking and obtaining permission from Fauquier to do so. Both of Ross's port engines were by now feathered, but at least they had stopped smoking. The front turret of Watts's Lancaster opened up at around 250 yards, and the two fighters broke away and disappeared. Ross was seen to ditch off the Norwegian coast, and he and his crew were then observed to climb out onto the wing and inflate their Mae Wests. Watts remained at the scene until his fuel situation forced him to leave, by which time he knew, that an Air Sea Rescue Warwick was on its way from Sumburgh. The Warwick took off at 14.43, and arrived a little over an hour later to find the Lancaster still afloat, but only just. By the time it had circled and dropped a lifeboat at 16.05, the Lancaster had disappeared beneath the waves, and the crew was in the water. In the fading light, one man was seen to be swimming towards the lifeboat, but the approach of an enemy fighter forced the Warwick crew to turn for home. Throughout the night Coastal Command Catalinas searched the sea right up to the Norwegian coast, one of them with a Leigh Light, but no trace was found of the Ross crew or the lifeboat. Three Warwicks and three Ansons continued the search on the following day with a fighter escort, but they also found nothing, and the search was called off as darkness fell. It is believed by some, that the enemy fighter seen earlier by the Warwick crew strafed and killed the unfortunate crewmembers.

W/C James Tait stands proudly behind his favoured Lancaster EE146 KC-D after the final attack on the *Tirpitz* on the 12th of November 1944.

Tait with his crew after returning from the third attack on the *Tirpitz*.

Three days after the sinking of the *Tirpitz* Secretary of State for Air, Sir Archibald Sinclair, is pictured congratulating W/C Tait and other participants in the operation.

On the 14th of November 1944 W/C Tait gave a press interview in London to tell the world about 617 Squadron's part in the sinking of the *Tirpitz* at its Norwegian mooring.

The beautiful and mighty battleship *Tirpitz*. Laid down in October 1936, the *Tirpitz*, sister ship of the *Bismarck*, represented a major leap forward in warship design, and was the means by which the Kriegsmarine intended to wrest control of the seas from the Royal Navy. She was launched in January 1939 in a blaze of publicity at a ceremony attended by Hitler himself and the entire Nazi hierarchy. An audience was transported to Wilhelmshaven from all over Germany to watch Frau von Hassel, the daughter of the man after whom the ship was named, perform the traditional act of breaking the champagne bottle over her bows. This she did with great reluctance and under pressure from the regime for which she had no sympathy. It was a further two years before *Tirpitz* was completed at a standard displacement of 41,700 tons, and with a main armament of eight fifteen inch guns. She had a design speed with a full load of thirty knots, and by 1944 a crew complement of more than nineteen hundred officers and men. At over eight hundred feet long *Tirpitz* was larger, faster, better armed and better protected than her British contemporaries, and these aspects alone would enable her to impact the war and British thinking without her ever engaging other surface vessels in combat at sea. The very fact that she existed, albeit for most of her career at her moorings in Norwegian fjords, was enough to keep Churchill and the Admiralty in a constant state of agitation. She had to be destroyed, and numerous attempts were made to penetrate her defences, some partially successful, others dismal failures. Bomber Command had last attacked the battleship in Norway at the end of April 1942, when a small force of Halifaxes and Lancasters from 4 and 5 Groups failed to inflict any damage, and the now A-O-C 8 Group, AVM Don Bennett, had been shot down and evaded capture. Other attempts were made by dive-bombers, manned torpedoes and X-craft (mini submarines), and while repairing the damage kept *Tirpitz* immobile, she was still a threat, an annoying itch that could not be ignored. As long as she remained afloat she would disproportionately occupy the minds of British war planners and tie up elements of the Royal Navy that were needed elsewhere.

S/L John Cockshott arrived at 617 Squadron from 1660 Conversion Unit as a Flight Lieutenant on the 30th of July 1944. He was immediately promoted to the rank of Squadron Leader and given the post of flight commander. He took part in his first operation with the squadron against U-Boot pens at La Pallice on the 11th of August 1944. He adopted PD238 as his personal Lancaster, and is pictured here, third from left, with his crew at Woodhall Spa after participating in the first *Tirpitz* operation.

Lt Nick Knilans poses for an official photograph with his crew. 617 Squadron undertook its final wartime change of address with a move from Coningsby to Woodhall Spa between the 7th and 9th of January 1944, while 619 Squadron went in the other direction. The officers were billeted in the elegant Petwood Hotel on the edge of the town, where it stands to this day resplendent in its extensive and beautiful grounds, while the NCOs were accommodated in Maycrete huts at nearby Tattershall Thorpe. Among new crews arriving on posting was that of the American Lt Knilans from 619 Squadron. Hubert "Nick" Knilans was to become one of 617 Squadron's characters, and unusually, he remained at Woodhall Spa for his entire operational career of two tours. Born in Wisconsin in 1917, Knilans joined the RCAF in October 1941, before America entered the war. After basic training as a pilot in Canada, Knilans arrived in the UK to continue his training, initially in Scotland, and then at 1660 CU at Swinderby. Here he gathered a crew around him, and was posted to 619 Squadron at Woodhall Spa in June 1943. In September Knilans was commissioned as a Pilot Officer, and in early October his rear gunner was killed by a night fighter during an operation to Kassel. Soon afterwards he was transferred to the USAAF, but was allowed to remain on attachment to the RAF, although sporting an American uniform in the rank of 1st Lieutenant.

The *Tirpitz* photographed in a Norwegian Fjord in October 1943.

A dramatic shot of Gibson flying over the shoreline at Reculver during the testing of *Upkeep* in May 1943. Gibson can just be made out sitting at the controls.

An earlier shot of the same sequence.

A fine shot of G/C "Johnny" Fauquier's Lancaster B1 Special PD119 YZ-J. The B1 Special was modified to accommodate the giant 22,000lb *Grand Slam*, big brother to the *Tallboy*. Uprated Merlin engines, a stronger undercarriage, the removal and fairing over of the mid-upper and front turrets and the removal of the bomb bay doors, together with a reduced five man crew enabled the remarkable Lancaster to carry the war's heaviest bomb and transport it to central Germany. Fauquier's aircraft had a black port tail fin for recognition purposes, so that other aircraft could formate on it.

The Wallis designed *Grand Slam*, the ultimate in shockwave technology. Dropped in anger for the first time on the 14th of March 1945 by S/L Jock Calder in PD112 against the Bielefeld Viaduct, it proved highly successful, and enjoyed further successes against the Arnsberg Viaduct, the Arbergen railway bridge and the Nienburg bridge over the Weser. *Grand Slam* was equally effective against concrete pens and those at Farge, Ijmuiden and Hamburg gave testimony to its destructive capability. The weapon was used for the final time against fortifications on the island of Heligoland on the 19th of April 1945, just a week before Bomber Command ceased heavy bomber operations.

Grand Slam's huge girth clearly visible.

An unofficial photograph of W/C Cheshire's Lancaster DV380 taken by engine fitter Basil Pearson at Woodhall Spa during the early months of 1944.

A Flight commander at 617 Squadron, William (Bill) Astell.

Karl Schütte stands at the back of this group at their flak position on the Möhne Dam. He was decorated for his part in bringing down Hopgood's Lancaster.

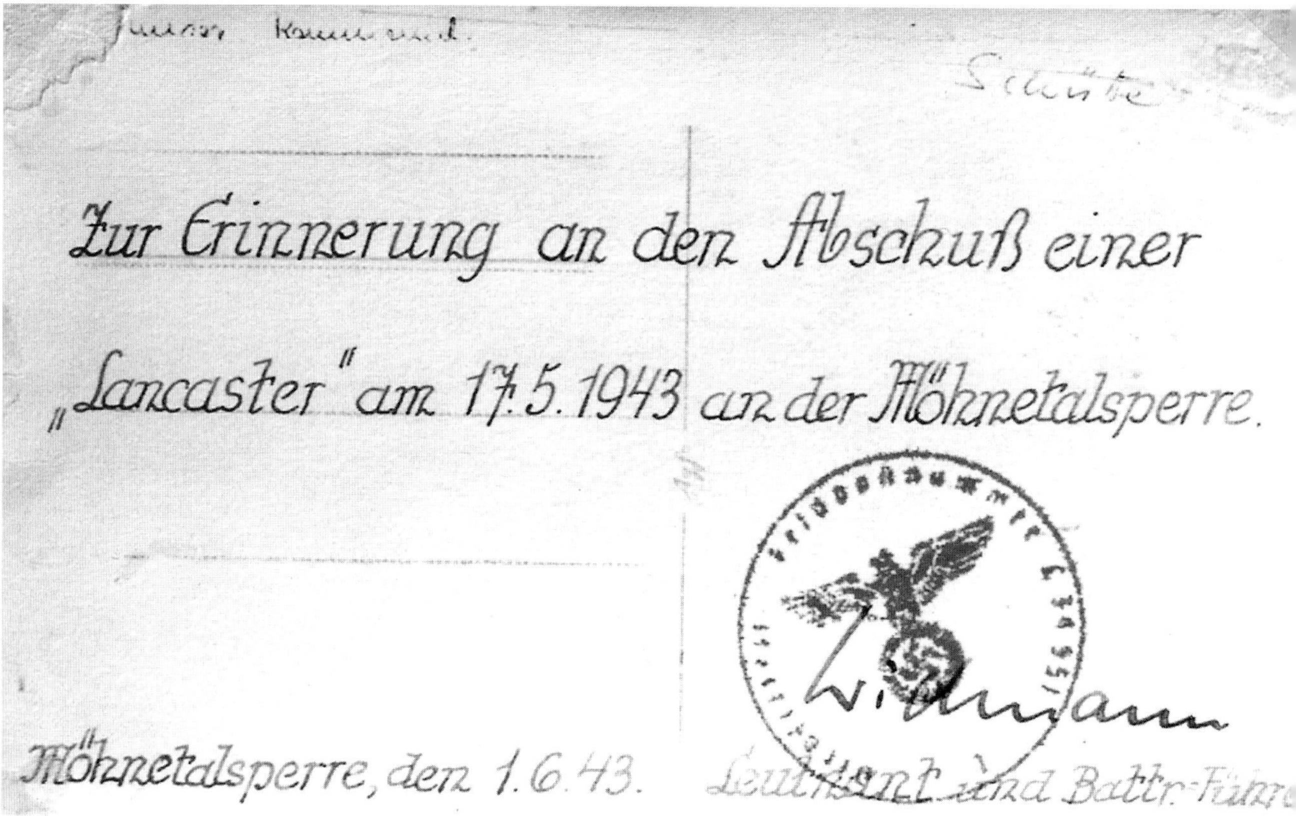

Lieber Kamerad.

Schütte

Zur Erinnerung an den Abschuß einer

"Lancaster" am 17.5.1943 an der Möhnetalsperre.

Möhnetalsperre, den 1.6.43.   *Leutnant und Battr.-Führer*

A certificate to commemorate Schütte's part in the defence of the Möhne Dam on the night of the 16/17th of May 1943. It reads, In memory of the shooting down of a Lancaster on the 17.5.43. on the Möhne Dam. It is dated the 1st of June 1943 and is signed by Leutnant Widmann, the battery commander.

The German military inspects the shattered remains of Hopgood's Lancaster ED925 AJ-M in a field near Ostönnen, six kilometres from the dam. The tail fin was one of the few recognisable pieces after the aircraft was torn apart in the air when the fuel tank exploded.

Karl Schütte with a propeller blade from ED925.

The Möhne Dam with the reservoir at full capacity. Dummy trees line the roadway in an effort to camouflage the structure. The torpedo nets hang from the flotation devices in front of the dam wall.

Texel is the most southerly of the Dutch Frisian Islands, and during the war it was the home to marine flak units that greeted Allied bombers on the way to Germany, and bade them a fond farewell on the way home. Many RAF bombers crashed on or near the Island, and the cemetery at Den Burg is the final resting place of more than a hundred. This photograph shows a Marine battery firing heavy shells at high-flying targets.

Another view of one of the flak positions on Texel showing the layout of the installation.

A close up of one of the gun barrels in its housing. In order to hit a very low flying aircraft it was necessary to position the barrel at its lowest elevation as in this shot, but even that could be too high.

Burpee, third from right, with five of his crew in front of their Lancaster while serving with 467 Squadron RAAF.

Les Knight and his crew relax on the scrub across the peritrack from the 617 Squadron hangar. From L-R navigator Hobday, bomb-aimer Johnson, front gunner Sutherland, pilot Knight, wireless operator Kellow (rear), rear gunner O'Brien and flight engineer Grayston. In the early hours of the 16th of September 1943, while searching in fog at low level for the aiming point on the banks of the Dortmund-Ems Canal, Knight's Lancaster JB144 struck trees and lost two engines. This, together with damaged control surfaces, dictated that the crew would not make it home. After jettisoning the 12,000lb "cookie" Knight struggled on towards Holland, and reached the town of Den Ham before it became necessary to abandon ship. Knight remained at the controls while his seven crew members parachuted to safety, but he knew that he could not reach an escape hatch before the aircraft flipped over. He tried to make a forced landing, but struck trees and crashed with fatal consequences in a field on the edge of the town. The local people honoured Knight with a funeral under the noses of the German occupiers and strictly against regulations.

A mobile crane stands on rails on the quayside of the Wet Triangle at Bergeshövede, the basin which acts as the meeting point for the Dortmund-Ems and Mittelland Canals. It was here that S/L Ralf Allsebrook and his crew crashed during the disastrous operation to bomb the banks of the Dortmund-Ems Canal on the night of the 15/16th of September 1943. On fire and already doomed, Lancaster EE130 bounced off the roof of a house, collided with the crane, knocking it into the water, flipped over and crashed into the Wet Triangle killing all on board. The bomb had already been jettisoned, and it is believed was recovered intact by the Germans. The crane proved to be undamaged, and was dragged from the water to be returned to service.

The German military recover the wreckage of Allsebrook's Lancaster AJ-A from the Wet Triangle on the morning of the 16th of September 1943. At the extreme left of the photo, halfway up, can be seen three figures standing on the quayside. One of these is Frau Erika Kaiser, who lives today as then on the water front. Her late husband was the battery commander of one of the units responsible for bringing Allsebrook down.

Another scene of the recovery of Allsebrook's Lancaster.

The Dortmund-Ems Canal operation of the 15/16th September 1943 involved eight Lancasters and crews from 617 Squadron, five of which failed to return. Among the missing was the crew of F/L Harold Wilson, who had trained for Operation *Chastise*, but were prevented through illness from taking part. Despite the conditions of poor visibility, Wilson found the target near Ladbergen, and was in the process of making a bombing run when his aircraft was engaged by flak. On fire, JA898 KC-X struck trees as Wilson sought to make a controlled landing. This photograph taken by a local resident clearly shows the damage to the treetops.

Wilson came down adjacent to the Canal, and the Lancaster burst into flames. It is believed that none of the eight occupants survived the impact. Some fifteen minutes later the 12,000lb "Cookie" detonated, and the photograph shows the result.

David and Georgina (Nina) Maltby pictured while he was serving at 97 Squadron at Woodhall Spa. Maltby and his crew lost their lives in tragic circumstances on the night of the 14/15th of September 1943, as they turned for home after a recall when bound for the Dortmund-Ems Canal. Maltby's body alone was recovered, and he was laid to rest in the church yard in Wickhambreux in Kent, where he and Nina were married.

Date	Hour	Aircraft Type and No.	Pilot	Duty	Remarks (Including results of bombing, gunnery, exercises, etc.)	Flying Times Day	Night
1·5·43	1145	LANC III 'B' ED 864/G	F/LT ASTELL	Nav.	Air Test, etc.	1:00	
6·5·43	1630	B	F/LT ASTELL	Nav.	Air Test, Bombing 4 Bombs Ht 60ft	0:55	
6·5·43	1940	B ED 864	F/LT ASTELL	Nav.	BASE-SELBY-HORNSEA-SYN 0100E-SHERINGHAM 9 runs.		3:30
			LOW LEVEL		LAKEn-COLCHESTER-TRING AFS-LAKEsw UPPINGHAM-BASE		
7·5·43	2030	B	F/LT ASTELL	Nav.	BASE-WAINFLEET-LAKE sw COLCHESTER-LAKE sw		2:00
			LOW LEVEL		UPPINGHAM-BASE. 4 Bombs. Ht 60ft. 1 run.		
9·5·43	2050	B	F/LT ASTELL	Nav.	BASE-WAINFLEET-LAKE sw UPPINGHAM-BASE		1:20
11·5·43	1936	B	F/LT ASTELL	Nav	BASE-CHESTERFIELD-DERWICK-BARNSLEY-WAINFLEET 4 Bombs 12 runs		3:15
					LAKE sw COLCHESTER-LANE UPPINGHAM-NEWARK-BASE		
13·5·43	1357	B	F/LT ASTELL	Nav	BASE-WAINFLEET-LAKE UPP.-NEWPORT-BASE 4Bombs	1:40	
13·5·43	1533	B	F/LT ASTELL	Nav	BASE-NEWPORT-LAKE UPP. WAINFLEET-BASE 4 Bombs	1:40	
14·5·43	2154	B.	"	Nav.	Exercises.		2:35
16·5·43	-	B	"	NAV.	"ORS" EDER MISSING		
					No. 617 Sqn.		
					Summary for May.		
					Day 5:15.	5:15	12:40
					Night 12:40.		
					Total 17:55		

S/L A ? (signature)

U/Cdr O617 Sqn (signature)

TOTAL TIME.... 258. / 207 . 00

The last page in the log book of Floyd Wile, the Canadian navigator in Astell's crew. The final entries have been written in a different hand and signed off by David Maltby.